W9-BWJ-362

SUPERSTARS
OF THE
INDIANAPOLIS
COLTS

by M.K. Osborne

AMICUS | AMICUS INK

Amicus High Interest and Amicus Ink are imprints of Amicus
P.O. Box 1329, Mankato, MN 56002
www.amicuspublishing.us

Library of Congress Cataloging-in-Publication Data
Names: Osborne, M. K., author.
Title: Superstars of the Indianapolis Colts / By M.K. Osborne.
Description: Mankato, MN : Amicus, [2019] | Series: Pro sports superstars NFL |
Includes index. | Audience: K to Grade 3.
Identifiers: LCCN 2017057275 (print) | LCCN 2018008032 (ebook) | ISBN 9781681514895
(pdf) | ISBN 9781681514079 (library binding) | ISBN 9781681523279 (pbk.)
Subjects: LCSH: Indianapolis Colts (Football team)--Biography--Juvenile literature. |
Indianapolis Colts (Football team)--History--Juvenile literature. | Football players--
United States--Biography--Juvenile literature.
Classification: LCC GV939.I53 (ebook) | LCC GV939.I53 .O73 2019 (print) | DDC
796.332/640977252--dc23
LC record available at https://lccn.loc.gov/2017057275

Photo Credits: All photos from Associated Press except Getty Images/Focus On Sport,
8–9; Newscom/iconphotosfour765053, 20–21

Series Designer: Veronica Scott
Book Designer: Ciara Beitlich/Veronica Scott
Photo Researcher: Holly Young

Printed in China
HC 10 9 8 7 6 5 4 3 2 1
PB 10 9 8 7 6 5 4 3 2 1

TABLE OF CONTENTS

GET TO KNOW THE COLTS

The Colts joined the **NFL** in 1953. They moved from Baltimore, Maryland, to Indianapolis, Indiana, in 1984. The Colts have won four NFL **titles**. They have won two Super Bowls.

Who are some of the Colts' greatest stars? Let's find out!

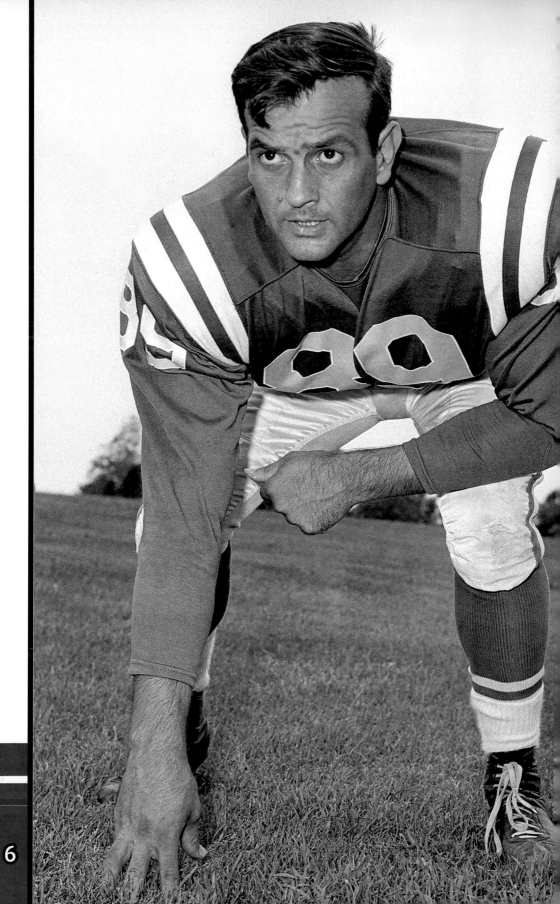

GINO MARCHETTI

Gino Marchetti was good at tackling. He hit hard. It took more than one man to block him. But he always played a fair game. Marchetti went to 11 **Pro Bowls** in a row. His first was in 1955.

RAYMOND BERRY

Raymond Berry was not the fastest runner. But he was clever. He joined the Colts in 1955. He only **fumbled** one time in 13 seasons. He played in six Pro Bowls.

Some called Unitas "The Golden Arm" because he was such a great passer.

JOHNNY UNITAS

Johnny Unitas was a **quarterback**. He was a star passer. Unitas won three NFL **MVP** awards. He helped the Colts win two NFL titles and one Super Bowl. Unitas was added to the NFL Hall of Fame in 1979.

MARVIN HARRISON

Marvin Harrison was on offense. He caught 143 passes in 2002. That is the most passes caught in one season by a Colt ever. He went to eight Pro Bowls. He helped the Colts win the Super Bowl in 2007.

PEYTON MANNING

Peyton Manning was a good leader. He joined the Colts in 1998. He led them to a Super Bowl win in 2007. He was named MVP four times with the Colts. He played on the team for 14 years.

ANDREW LUCK

Andrew Luck is a smart quarterback. He joined the team in 2012. Luck set a record for passing as a **rookie**. He has been to three Pro Bowls.

The Colts chose Luck first overall in the 2012 NFL draft.

T.Y. HILTON

T.Y. Hilton is great at catching passes. He joined the Colts in 2012. He has been to three Pro Bowls. He once caught 13 passes within 224 yards.

YOUNG STAR

Malik Hooker is on defense. He played on the Ohio State football team. The Colts chose him in the first round of the 2017 draft. He is good at making **interceptions**.

Let's watch and see who will be the next star of the Colts!

TEAM FAST FACTS

Founded: 1953 (as the Baltimore Colts)

Home Stadium: Lucas Oil Statium (Indianapolis, Indiana)

Super Bowl Titles: 2 (1971 and 2007)

NFL Titles: 3 (1958, 1959 and 1968)

Hall of Fame Players: 9 including Gino Marchetti, Raymond Berry, Johnny Unitas, and John Mackey

WORDS TO KNOW

fumble – to drop or lose control of the football

interception – when a player catches a pass from the other team's quarterback allowing their own team to get possession of the ball

MVP – Most Valuable Player; an honor given to the best player each season

NFL – National Football League; a group that organizes and promotes pro football games

Pro Bowl – the NFL's all-star game

quarterback – a player whose main jobs are to lead the offense and throw passes

title – a championship

LEARN MORE

Books

Adamson, Thomas K. *The Indianapolis Colts Story*. Minneapolis: Bellwether Media, 2017.

Murray, Laura K. *Andrew Luck*. Mankato, Minn.: Creative Education, 2017.

Websites

Indianapolis Colts—Official Site
http://www.colts.com
Watch video clips and view photos of the Indianapolis Colts.

NFL Rush
http://www.nflrush.com
Play games and learn how to be a part of NFL PLAY 60.

NFL.com
http://nfl.com
Check out pictures and your favorite football players' stats.

Every effort has been made to ensure that these websites are appropriate for children. However, because of the nature of the Internet, it is impossible to guarantee that these sites will remain active indefinitely or that their contents will not be altered.

INDEX